BAD BLOOD

NORTH POINT
RESOURCES

[CONTENTS]

USING THE PARTICIPANT'S GUIDE

[BEFORE SESSION ONE]

1. Read through *A Typical Group Meeting* below to gain an understanding of the flow of this study.

2. Read through the content in *Session One* on pages 9–12.

[A TYPICAL GROUP MEETING]

1. Turn to the *Notes* page, and watch the video segment.

2. Use the *Discussion Questions* to have a conversation about the video content.

3. Read the *Think About It* section aloud.

4. Review the *Before the Next Session* homework at the end of the chapter.

Social Time	30 minutes
Video	20 minutes
Discussion	55 minutes
Prayer	15 minutes

[INTRODUCTION]

Let me tell you a story about my family. My older sister is in a biracial relationship with a guy who was born in Jamaica and grew up in the Bronx. For months, their relationship was great. His relationship with our family was great. And then something happened that introduced bad blood.

My sister and her boyfriend were watching my kids, and her boyfriend said to my three-year-old, "Hey kids, I heard you guys got a new hot tub. I can't wait to come over and see it."

Here's how my three-year-old responded: "We don't let people with dark skin in our hot tub."

Later, when my sister told me this story, my heart sank. I was mortified. I was confused. I was even frustrated and angry with Jake. In our family, we don't talk like that about people. We believe *every person* is made in God's image. Where did Jake hear something like that, and why did he repeat it? The truth is, three-year-olds sometimes say things they don't understand. I had a conversation with Jake and, as far as I can tell, he just made up what he said out of the blue. He had no understanding of how hurtful it was.

But the damage had been done. Feelings had been hurt. The relationship had been tainted by bad blood. It was going to take effort to put things right. It was going to be awkward.

I'm so excited that you're about to embark on this four-week study. The topic of bad blood touches all of our lives. It's everywhere. We all have relationships that are tainted by it. Maybe it's a co-worker that heats up lasagna in the microwave and makes the entire office smell like garlic. Maybe it's a family member with whom you're no longer on speaking terms. You find yourself concocting holiday plans to make sure you avoid him or her. Maybe bad blood found its way into your marriage, and you're wondering if you can keep the vows you made on your wedding day.

We all have bad blood in our lives. It's part of the human condition.

This study isn't just for people in epically bad relationships. Those kinds of relationships exist, and they're awful. But this study is also for anyone who has a relationship that's difficult. Here's what I know is true about bad blood: without warning, it can enter even the healthiest and most normal relationships. I don't want that for you.

I pray *Bad Blood* gives you information and tools to make your relationships better.

SESSION ONE

[THE EMPATHY LENS]

In Romans 12:18, the apostle Paul wrote, "If it is possible, as far as it depends on you, live at peace with everyone." That's easier said than done, right? But before you dismiss Paul's advice, consider that when he wrote those words, he was up to his eyeballs in bad blood.

Early in his career, Paul made a name for himself by persecuting Christians. He had them imprisoned and even oversaw their executions. But all of that changed when he had a personal experience with Jesus (you can read about it in Acts 9). Almost overnight, he went from hating the movement Jesus had started to being one of its greatest leaders. He planted churches all over the Mediterranean rim. The letters he wrote to those churches eventually became more than half of the writings that make up what we call the New Testament.

But when you make a sudden life change like Paul did, it doesn't automatically create trust in the people around you—especially the people you've hurt. Paul was trying to build relationships with people he had imprisoned. In some cases, he was trying to build relationships with the families of people who had been killed because of his actions. Can you imagine what Paul's conversion was like for those people? Can you imagine how difficult it must have been for them to see him move into a position of leadership and influence in the church?

Paul's old friends were probably confused as well. They saw the church as a dangerous movement that challenged all of the traditions they held sacred. They thought Paul agreed with them, and then all of a sudden he was advocating everything they disliked about Christianity.

Paul knew what it was like to try to live at peace with everyone. He had bad blood on both sides of his conversion to Christianity. He had given nearly everyone in his life a reason to dislike and distrust him. But he understood an important truth: *Lack of peace about any relationship will rob you of peace in your own life.*

YOU DO YOU

If you have a relationship that's characterized by bad blood, you may never find peace. But the pursuit of peace is worthwhile, even if you never find it. In Romans 12:18, Paul didn't urge us to simply live at peace with everyone. He didn't treat bad blood as though it's easy to resolve. It's important to recognize that the verse begins with, "If it is possible, as far as it depends on you . . ."

Sometimes, peace isn't possible. When it comes to doing away with bad blood in a relationship, there are factors you can't control. Paul understood that. The verse isn't really a command to live in peace; it's encouragement to live in a way that maximizes the potential for peace.

Have you ever heard someone say, "You do you"? It's a colloquial phrase that means, "Just be yourself." It's a reminder that you are the only person you're in charge of. When it comes to your relationships, you are the variable you can control. Other people may not choose to live at peace with you, but you can choose to live as though peace is possible.

When it comes to peace in your relationships, what depends on you? In any relationship, you have to own your piece of the pie. You have to say, "I said that and I shouldn't have" or "I did that and I shouldn't have." If you have bad blood in a relationship, it may be mostly the other person's fault. But even if it's small, you still have a piece of the pie. You've still contributed to the bad blood in some way. It's important to own your part. *That* is what depends on you. You can't control the behavior of others, but you can control your behavior. You do you.

Maybe you feel like you've gone as far as you can to repair a relationship. Take a closer look. Are you sure you can't go any further? Maybe you feel like you've done everything you can do. Take a closer look. Is there something else you can do?

Maybe you're wondering, *When is enough, enough? Is it ever irresponsible for me to continue in a bad-blood relationship?* For the answer to that question, stick around. We'll talk about that in the sessions to come. But in this session, we want to explore one step we can all take in our bad-blood relationships, regardless of the details of our circumstances.

We can *pursue empathy*.

Empathy is different than sympathy. Sympathy is acknowledging what another person feels. Empathy is stepping into another person's pain. It involves feeling what he or she feels. That's not easy. It's not natural. It's not quick. But it is first aid to the bad blood in your life.

You may never have peace in a bad-blood relationship, but if you choose the path of empathy, you can have peace *about* that relationship.

There are four steps to pursuing empathy, according to Dr. Brené Brown, author of *Rising Strong: The Reckoning. The Rumble. The Revolution.*

1. Take on the other person's perspective—try to put yourself in that person's shoes.
2. Suspend your judgment—you have your perspective on the bad blood; put that perspective aside for the time being.
3. Recognize the other person's emotion—accept what that person feels as a result of the bad blood, even if you think those feelings aren't valid or realistic.
4. Communicate that emotion—articulate what the other person feels.

NOTES

DISCUSSION QUESTIONS

1. Talk about a relationship in your life that you value and appreciate. What are some things about that relationship that make your life better?

2. When have you witnessed bad blood entering a relationship between two people? How did the people respond? What was the outcome?

3. If empathy is "feeling what another person feels," do you think our culture values empathy? Why or why not?

4. Read Romans 12:18 below. What are some negative feelings, attitudes, or behaviors you tend to contribute to your relationships? How do those feelings, attitudes, or behaviors make it difficult for you to live at peace with others?

    > *If it is possible, as far as it depends on you, live at peace with everyone.* Romans 12:18

5. What are some possible risks of following Jesus by taking the long walk of empathy in a bad-blood relationship in your life? Do those risks make it difficult for you to believe that empathy is worth the effort? Why or why not?

6. Are you currently struggling with a bad-blood relationship? If so, what can you do between now and the next session to take on the other person's perspective? How can this group help you?

THINK ABOUT IT

Jesus is the most dramatic example of God's empathy. God didn't have to go out of his way to demonstrate that he feels what we feel—but he did. He sent his only Son to live among us and experience the things we experience, both good and bad. Jesus was crucified and raised from the dead so we could reconnect relationally with our heavenly Father. In that history-changing act, Jesus demonstrated the power of empathy and forgiveness to overcome bad blood.

God asks us to forgive others as he forgave us. He asks us to love others as he loves us. He asks us to show mercy to others, just as he showed mercy to us. When we take the long walk of empathy, we mirror what God did for us. It's not easy to take on another person's perspective, suspend judgment, recognize another person's emotion, and communicate that emotion. When we do that, it feels like we're letting the other person off the hook for the ways he or she wronged us. And when we're wronged, we don't want to offer forgiveness. We want justice. We want payback.

But through Jesus' death, God paid back what we owed *him*. He paid the price on our behalf. He put aside our bad blood at enormous personal cost.

Maintaining our anger with someone requires energy. That energy tends to spill out in all of our relationships. Our kids, family, friends, and co-workers end up carrying the weight of our bitterness. Holding onto anger—even when it's justified—can poison all of our relationships. That's why it's important to listen to Paul's wisdom in Romans 12:18 and then act on it:

If it is possible, as far as it depends on you, live at peace with everyone.

15

BEFORE THE NEXT SESSION

Read pages 17–20 for an overview of next session's content.

SESSION TWO

[HOLDING ON]

Last session, we talked about the power of empathy in breaking bad blood's hold on a relationship. Sometimes, when you consider the other person's perspective, you realize that he or she is broken. The other person isn't just hurtful; he or she is also hurting. That doesn't undo the pain the person has caused. It doesn't make everything right. The bad news is that it doesn't necessarily fix the problems in the relationship. The good news is that it gives you a new and healthier perspective on the relationship.

Just because you reach out with empathy doesn't mean past wrongs are righted or that the other person has changed. Sometimes, even when you reach out with empathy, the other person keeps hurting you. Maybe that person doesn't care. Maybe he or she doesn't know any better. Maybe he or she can't help it. Whatever the situation or excuse, it doesn't ease your pain.

That pain usually finds its way into your other relationships. Friends, family, and co-workers walk on eggshells around you. They sense your anger. It comes out in your mood and tone of voice. It makes you less willing to fully invest in relationships because you're keenly aware of the risks. You think that if one person hurt you, others will too.

The goal of this study is to help you begin to find peace—not only in your bad-blood relationships, but in *all* of your relationships. Finding peace leads to personal freedom, greater satisfaction, and more joy. It's the life Jesus wants for you.

The path to peace is paved with empathy, but the vehicle to get us there is forgiveness.

SETTING THE PRISONER FREE

In his book *Forgive and Forget*, Lewis B. Smedes said, "To forgive is to set a prisoner free and discover that the prisoner was you." When you refuse to forgive, you let past wrongs lurk in your mind and heart. Too often, you pay the price for your lack of forgiveness. That's because bad blood costs you peace and complicates your other relationships.

Last session, we looked at Romans 12:18. The apostle Paul wrote, "If it is possible, as far as it depends on you, live at peace with everyone." In the very next verse, he says the following:

> Do not take revenge, my dear friends, but leave room for God's wrath, for it is written: "It is mine to avenge; I will repay, says the Lord." Romans 12:19

For some people, revenge is keying someone's car. For others, it is shutting someone out of their lives for a season or maybe even indefinitely. But revenge isn't just retaliating against someone who hurt you. It's also celebrating another person's misfortune. Sometimes, it's getting back at someone directly. Sometimes, it's being happy when something bad happens to him or her.

He had to go to the emergency room because he drank too much?
Oh, that's too bad.

She lost her job because she was late to work one time too many?
That's so sad.

As long as we celebrate others' misfortunes—even the misfortunes of those who have harmed us—we're not free. That's because revenge escalates. It causes us to suspend our morality. It tempts us to compromise. Over time, it changes who we are and how we relate to God and others.

Let's talk about the next part of the verse: "but leave room for God's wrath." That sounds scary, right? Or, if you have a bad-blood relationship in your life, maybe you're thinking, *Now we're talking!* But what does Paul mean when he writes about God's wrath?

Wrath is God's reaction to sin. We can't fully understand it because we only know our own wrath, but God's wrath is perfect. It's justified. And it tells us something about his character. God doesn't deal lightly with sin. He doesn't shrug his shoulders and give an enigmatic smile in the face of pain and cruelty. God cares. He's offended by pain and cruelty. He made us in his image and wrote his law on our hearts, which is why we have consciences. It's why we have an innate sense of right and wrong, of justice and injustice. Our cruelty disturbs God. It stirs his wrath.

Because God cares, sin is never without consequences. It's like Las Vegas: the house always wins. Sin will always make you pay. When someone's sin harms you, it may look like he or she is getting away with it. But no one gets away with it. Maybe that person hurt you because he's looking for purpose and meaning in all the wrong places. Maybe that person hurt you because she's chasing something she'll never have and wouldn't even want if she understood the cost of the chase.

One way or another, sin has consequences. That's why empathy paves the way to peace. By taking on the other person's perspective, you can begin to see the toll that sin is taking in his or her life. That perspective leads to compassion and opens the door to forgiveness. When we "leave room for God's wrath," we're trusting that our heavenly Father will respond to the person's sin with the appropriate combination of grace, mercy, and even wrath—because he loves that person more than we ever could.

Choosing to not forgive another person is a failure to believe what God says. If you believe there is a God, why not believe that he is God and you are not? It's his job to repay, not yours. So, what does forgiveness look like? How would you treat someone who hurt you if you were fully confident it was God's job to repay as he saw fit? Paul explains in Romans 12:20. Be warned: his approach (which quotes wisdom from the book of Proverbs) is radical. It's not our normal response to people who have wronged us.

> *On the contrary:*

> *"If your enemy is hungry, feed him; if he is thirsty, give him something to drink. In doing this, you will heap burning coals on his head."*

It means accepting the apology you'll never receive. It means trusting God. Peace begins when your demand for payment ends.

NOTES

DISCUSSION QUESTIONS

1. When someone wrongs you, do you tend to hold a grudge or get over it quickly? How does that tendency affect your relationships?

2. Has your relationship with someone ever been affected by his or her bad blood with someone else? How did the person's bad blood make things difficult for you? What did you do?

3. When someone wrongs you, do you think it's realistic to "leave room for God's wrath"? Why or why not?

4. Read Romans 12:17–19 below. Think about a bad-blood relationship in your life. If you choose to trust God and move toward empathy and forgiveness, what do you think it might cost you?

    > Do not repay anyone evil for evil. Be careful to do what is right in the eyes of everyone. If it is possible, as far as it depends on you, live at peace with everyone. Do not take revenge, my dear friends, but leave room for God's wrath, for it is written: "It is mine to avenge; I will repay," says the Lord. Romans 12:17–19

5. Is there someone you need to forgive—even if that person doesn't want your forgiveness? How do you think moving toward forgiveness might improve your quality of life and have a positive effect on your other relationships?

6. What is one thing you can do before the next session to take a step toward forgiveness in your bad-blood relationship? How can this group support you?

THINK ABOUT IT

What about your bad blood? What do you do?

Maybe you need to accept an apology you previously rejected. Maybe you need to accept an apology you never received. Doing so might offer the other person the forgiveness he or she never received, which may have led to choices that hurt others.

Maybe you need to ask God for the wisdom and strength to trust him with outcomes. Maybe someone hurt you so deeply that you need to ask your heavenly Father what taking a first step toward forgiveness even looks like for you.

Don't let bad blood overcome you. Don't let it rob you of peace. Understand that you can forgive without condoning. You can let go of what that person owes you without losing yourself. In fact, letting go and trusting God is the only way to find peace.

Forgive the debt. Take the first step. That may begin with:

- Writing a letter
- Making a phone call
- Sending a text message

BEFORE THE NEXT SESSION

Read pages 25–28 for an overview of next session's content.

SESSION THREE

[A CONFRONTATION OR A CONVERSATION]

Last session, we said that forgiveness is the vehicle to move you down the path toward peace. We urged you to take a first step toward forgiving a debt. But that often requires managing conflict in new ways. What does that look like? When you're at odds with another person, what should you do?

When there's bad blood in a relationship, the easiest thing to do is to let resentment and bitterness grow without addressing the issue. That's the path of least resistance. It doesn't make the conflict go away, but it avoids the relational mess of having to deal with the other person. Jesus calls his followers to a higher standard.

In Matthew 18:15, he says:

> "If your brother or sister sins, go and point out their fault, just between the two of you. If they listen to you, you have won them over."

That may sound simple at first. But the more you consider it, the more intimidating it becomes. Who enjoys going to someone and pointing out his or her fault? That's a recipe for hurt feelings, anger, and rejection. What are the odds the person will actually listen? Chances are, you won't win him or her over.

In this session, we're going to dig deeper into Jesus' advice. We'll look at his answers to three questions:

1. Why should you go to the other person?
2. When should you go to the other person?
3. How should you go to the other person?

Understanding the importance of those questions will help you push past the discomfort of potential anger and rejection in order to take a first step toward resolving bad blood between you and another person.

WHY, WHEN, AND HOW

For most of us, our natural instinct is to avoid conflict. If we have a problem with someone, it seems easiest to ignore it or to quietly let our anger fester into self-righteous bitterness. It should come as no surprise that Jesus offers a different approach—one that's counterintuitive and a bit scary. If you're familiar with Jesus, that's probably not a surprise. He has a way of raising the standard on everything.

In Matthew chapters 5 and 18, Jesus explains what to do about the bad blood in our lives. In Matthew 18, he tells us to go and have a conversation with the other person. In Matthew 5, he gives more detail about what that looks like.

> *"Therefore, if you are offering your gift at the altar and there remember that your brother or sister has something against you, leave your gift there in front of the altar. First go and be reconciled to them; then come and offer your gift."* Matthew 5:23–24

In Jesus' culture, there was one altar. It was in Jerusalem. Getting there took most people time and effort. The journey wasn't easy. It was setting a high standard to expect people to drop what they were doing and go make peace in their relationships before offering their gifts at the altar. To Jesus' audience, it must have sounded extreme and unrealistic.

Jesus' point is important. We think that in order to connect with God, we need to make things right with him. But before we can make things right with God, we have to make things right with others. That's because God loves all people. We can't have bad blood with others and fully connect with God.

Why should you go and make peace with the other person? Jesus says not making peace affects your connection to God.

Jesus' command is simple: Go! When you've wronged someone, take the first step. When someone has wronged you, *still* go take the first step.

When should you go and try to make peace with the other person? According to Jesus, you should do it right away. You should definitely do it before you try to make things right with God. If that sounds ridiculous, you're beginning to understand how important an idea it is.

Now, let's talk about *how* you should go to the other person.

Over the last two sessions, we discussed how you should approach the other person when you've been wronged. You build empathy by taking on the other person's perspective, suspending your judgment, recognizing the other person's emotions, and communicating an understanding of his or her feelings. Building empathy clears the path for forgiveness.

Forgiveness isn't about making things right. It's about letting go of what that person owes you. Forgiving isn't contingent on the other person. It doesn't matter whether he or she wants to be forgiven. Forgiveness is you writing off the debt by choosing not to hold it against that person. It might not change him or her, but it removes a weight from you and gets you on the path to finding peace *about* the relationship, even if you can't find peace *in* the relationship.

But how should you go to the other person when you're in the wrong? You can only make it right by confessing you are wrong. The Bible calls that *repenting*. It means you acknowledge the wrong you've done and choose not to do it again.

Repenting is a genuine change of heart. It's not saying things like, "I'm sorry if I offended you," "I can't imagine that hurt your feelings, but if it did I'm sorry," or, "I didn't realize you were so sensitive." Those kinds of apologies put the blame for the bad blood on the wronged person's emotions or reactions.

True repentance has three steps:

1. Take full responsibility for the wrong you've done.
2. Make no excuses for your behavior.
3. Lay out a plan for how you will change.

True repentance requires thought and effort. It also requires empathy. You'll have to put yourself in the other person's shoes, take responsibility, and come up with a workable plan for change.

NOTES

DISCUSSION QUESTIONS

1. How comfortable are you with confronting someone who has wronged you? How comfortable are you with apologizing to someone you've wronged? How do you think those tendencies affect the quality of your relationships?

2. As a group, take a few minutes to make a list of reasons people avoid confrontation. When you're finished, look through your list. How many of the items are about concern for the other person? How many of the items are about personal comfort or self-interest?

3. Read Matthew 5:23–24 below. Has your bad blood with another person ever affected your relationship with God? If so, how?

    "Therefore, if you are offering your gift at the altar and there remember that your brother or sister has something against you, leave your gift there in front of the altar. First go and be reconciled to them; then come and offer your gift." Matthew 5:23–24

4. Read Matthew 18:15 below. Respond to Jesus' command. Does it seem realistic? Why or why not?

    "If your brother or sister sins, go and point out their fault, just between the two of you. If they listen to you, you have won them over." Matthew 18:15

5. Is there a person to whom you need to repent because of the hurt you've caused? If so, what can you do before the next session to take full responsibility, make no excuses, and lay out a plan for change?

6. Is there someone with whom you need to have a conversation? What steps can you take before the next session to go and have that conversation? How can this group support you?

THINK ABOUT IT

Reconciliation requires turning a confrontation into a conversation. This isn't easy, but it doesn't mean you have a problem. Conflict and tension aren't signs that a relationship is broken. But if conflict festers, resentment can eventually poison the connection. There's always a cost associated with conflict, but the cost is even greater when we ignore hurt and pretend conflict doesn't exist.

Peace is not the same as the absence of conflict. Peace means navigating conflict in healthy ways that allow the relationship to move forward.

If you have bad blood in your life:

- Keep short accounts—don't wait to have a conversation with the other person.
- Keep it between the two of you—gossip doesn't heal bad blood.
- Keep in mind that you might not be right—sometimes, being humble and empathetic makes us realize that we own a bigger piece of the bad-blood pie than we initially thought.

BEFORE THE NEXT SESSION

Read pages 33–36 for an overview of next session's content.

[SHAKING THE DUST OFF]

No matter how badly you may want peace, there are some relationships that will never be fully resolved. That's because, as Marvin Gaye said, "It takes two, baby." For every wrong you repent of, there is someone else who must choose to forgive. For every wrong you forgive, there is someone else who must choose to repent. That may never happen. You can only control your choices and behavior. You can't control the other person.

The good news is that if you've done what depends on you, you can have peace about the relationship, even if you can't have peace in the relationship.

> *If it is possible, as far as it depends on you, live at peace with everyone.* Romans 12:18

As far as it depends on you, you make the effort. Each time there is an opportunity, you make the effort. You consistently reach out with repentance or forgiveness. You're always there to help the other person.

But is there a certain point at which continuing to extend assistance becomes irresponsible? Is there a point at which it actually becomes harmful to you? At what point does hope for the restoration of a relationship become delusional? When can we, as Jesus commanded in Matthew 10:14, shake the dust from our shoes and put some distance between us and people who are willfully stubborn?

What about when someone always wants to borrow money or live in your home? What about when someone continually says hurtful things to you? What about when someone has too much control over you or consistently takes advantage of your good intentions and desire for reconciliation?

In this session, we're going to explore the part of peace that doesn't depend on you. Instead, we'll look at the part that depends on the other person.

BURDEN VERSUS LOAD

Isn't it the good Christian way to continue to extend help to others in an attempt to reconcile bad-blood relationships? Not always. Unfortunately, there are toxic people. You may have bad blood with someone who is toxic. The Bible calls these people fools.

Foolish people continually behave in ways that are harmful to themselves or others. They don't take ownership of their behavior and choices. They refuse to take responsibility for their actions. They don't change their behavior to meet the demands of life. They expect reality to change in order to accommodate their needs and desires.

Proverbs 26:11 puts it this way: *As a dog returns to its vomit, so fools repeat their folly.*

When a fool's irresponsibility causes you harm, it's time to create boundaries in the relationship. Boundaries delineate what depends on you and what depends on the other person. They define what you're responsible for and what the other person is responsible for.

In his letter to the Galatians, the apostle Paul tells us how to know what depends on us and what depends on the other person.

> *Brothers and sisters, if someone is caught in a sin, you who live by the Spirit should restore that person gently. But watch yourselves, or you also may be tempted. Carry each other's burdens, and in this way you will fulfill the law of Christ. If anyone thinks they are something when they are not, they deceive themselves. Each one should test their own actions. Then they can take pride in themselves alone, without comparing themselves to someone else, for each one should carry their own load.* Galatians 6:1–5

If you follow Jesus, Paul's words are an assignment. They aren't optional. Jesus called us to love our neighbors as ourselves. That means we carry one another's burdens. A burden is any excessive weight. It's anything that's too big for one person to carry on his or her own. A job loss, the death of a family member, a cancer diagnosis—these things can be burdens. They can overwhelm and become too big for a person to carry on his or her own. Jesus calls us to come alongside those people and help them carry their burdens.

In the second half of the passage, Paul introduces the idea of personal responsibility. He calls each of us to test our own actions. That means honestly examining our lives and keeping a lookout for areas where we need to grow or change. It means asking ourselves, *Am I doing what I need to be doing?* That's because we should never ask someone to help us carry a burden we aren't carrying ourselves.

35

On the flip side of bearing one another's burdens is carrying our own loads. This sounds contradictory, but there's an important distinction: a burden is excess; a load is our portion. We each need to make sure we're carrying whatever it is that has been given to us to carry. It may be our emotions, attitudes, or behavior. It may be the way we respond to others. We're all responsible for our own loads. No one else can be responsible for your load.

Fools expect others to carry their burdens *and* their loads. Fools try to make others feel guilty for not helping them with their loads. But when we carry other people's loads, we rob them of experiencing the consequences of their decisions. You may be responsible for being a good neighbor, but you're not responsible for mowing your neighbor's grass.

To avoid carrying someone else's load:

1. Set boundaries.
2. Be accountable to someone.

Setting a boundary means asking the question, *Would it be better for me to love this person from a distance?* Being accountable means inviting someone into your struggle who can see things objectively and remind you that choosing not to give in to someone who wants you to carry his or her load doesn't mean you're giving up on that relationship.

NOTES

DISCUSSION QUESTIONS

1. Talk about a time when the negative consequences of your behavior taught you a valuable lesson. How do you think your life might be different if someone had helped you avoid those consequences?

2. Do you find it more difficult to offer others help or to receive help from others? How do you think that tendency has affected your relationships?

3. Read Galatians 6:1–5 below. Talk about a time when someone helped you carry a burden. How did that experience change your relationship with that person? How did it affect your relationship with God?

    > Brothers and sisters, if someone is caught in a sin, you who live by the Spirit should restore that person gently. But watch yourselves, or you also may be tempted. Carry each other's burdens, and in this way you will fulfill the law of Christ. If anyone thinks they are something when they are not, they deceive themselves. Each one should test their own actions. Then they can take pride in themselves alone, without comparing themselves to someone else, for each one should carry their own load. Galatians 6:1–5

4. Have you ever had to wrestle with the question of whether your assistance to someone was doing that person more harm than good? If so, what happened?

5. Is there a relationship in your life in which reconciliation seems impossible? If so, what can you do to begin to set healthy boundaries in that relationship? How can this group hold you accountable?

THINK ABOUT IT

You can have peace *about* a relationship, even if you don't have peace in the relationship. In fact, God wants peace for you. But you won't passively find peace. You have to pursue it.

What Jesus did on the cross is God's refusal to give up on his people. It's his refusal to give up on us. In return, Jesus asks us to follow his lead by loving others as he loved us, showing others mercy as he showed us mercy, and forgiving others as God forgave us. When it comes to the bad blood in our lives, Jesus calls us to make every effort to live at peace with one another. Making peace with others clears a path to peace with God.

Because God never gave up on us, we should never give up on others. But we also have to remember that we're no one's savior. There is a Savior. His name is Jesus. You be you, and let Jesus be Jesus.

[LEADER'S GUIDE]

[USING THE VIDEO AND PARTICIPANT'S GUIDE]

1. Socialize (30 minutes)
2. Watch Video (20 minutes)
3. Discuss Questions (55 minutes)
4. Pray (15 minutes)

[LEADING THE SESSIONS]

SESSION 1

Bad blood can infect any relationship. And the quality of our lives is only as good as the quality of our relationships. Lack of peace about a relationship robs you of peace in your own life. But you can have peace *about* a relationship even without peace *in* the relationship. Empathy is first aid for bad blood. When you empathize with someone, you see things you wouldn't have seen otherwise. Your anger turns to compassion. Your hurt begins to heal. You live out the kind of radical love to which Jesus called us. The Discussion Questions in this section are designed to help you and your group members consider what makes relationships good or bad, explore the power of empathy, and talk honestly about why being empathetic toward others is difficult.

SESSION 2

What do you do when you have bad blood with someone who owes you something? If you don't find peace in that relationship, your other relationships will suffer. In this session, you'll explore the topic of forgiveness. You'll talk about what it looks like to stop trying to make others pay what they owe you and surrender control to God. You will discuss important applications of the message. Who do you need to forgive? What does a first step toward forgiveness look like for you? What are the things that stand in the way of trusting God with outcomes and consequences in your bad-blood relationships?

SESSION 3

When there's bad blood in a relationship, the easiest thing to do is to let resentment and bitterness grow without addressing the issue. That's the path of least resistance. It doesn't make the conflict go away, but it avoids the relational mess of having to deal with the other person. Jesus calls his followers to a higher standard. He says that if we have a problem with another person, we should go and have a conversation with him or her. In this session, you'll discuss why you should go, when you should go, and how you should go.

SESSION 4

The first step to finding peace in a relationship is to repent if you've done wrong or to forgive if you've been wronged. But no matter how badly you want peace, there are some relationships that may never be fully restored. What do you do to find peace about a relationship when you can't find peace in the relationship? In this session, you'll discuss how God holds us responsible for helping carry others' burdens. He doesn't hold us responsible for carrying others' loads. When we carry another person's load, we rob that person of experiencing the outcomes of his or her decisions. You'll talk about the importance of setting boundaries in your relationships and being accountable to someone.

[GENERAL LEADER TIPS]

If you are the lead facilitator of the *Discussion Questions,* here are three things to consider during your group meetings:

CULTIVATE DISCUSSION

It is the ideas of everyone in the group that make a group meeting successful. Your role as the facilitator is to create an environment in which people feel safe to share their thoughts.

STAY ON TRACK

While you want to leave space for group members to think through the discussion, make sure the conversation is contributing to that session's topic. Don't let it veer off on tangents. Go with the flow, but be ready to nudge the conversation in the right direction when necessary.

PRAY

This is the most important thing you can do as a group. Pray that God is not only present at your group meetings, but that he is directing them.

NOTES

NOTES

NOTES

NOTES

NOTES